FEB 1 8 2021

3 1994 01605 5029

SANTA ANA PUBLIC LIBRARY

D0609283

J 523.45 FOX
Foxe, Steve
Jupiter

$29.32
CENTRAL   31994016055029

JUPITER

by Steve Foxe

PEBBLE
a capstone imprint

Pebble Explore is published by Pebble, an imprint of Capstone.
1710 Roe Crest Drive, North Mankato, Minnesota 56003
www.capstonepub.com

Copyright © 2021 by Capstone. All rights reserved. No part of this
publication may be reproduced in whole or in part, or stored in a retrieval
system, or transmitted in any form or by any means, electronic, mechanical,
photocopying, recording, or otherwise, without written permission of the
publisher.

**Library of Congress Cataloging-in-Publication Data is available on the
Library of Congress website.**
ISBN 978-1-9771-2395-4 (hardcover)
ISBN 978-1-9771-2695-5 (paperback)
ISBN 978-1-9771-2432-6 (eBook PDF)

Summary: Everything about Jupiter is big! Its size is big. Even its storms
are big! Get the big and small facts about this gas giant that can be seen
glowing in the night sky.

Image Credits
NASA: Enhanced image by Jason Major (CC-BY) based on images
provided courtesy of NASA/JPL-Caltech/SwRI/MSSS, 20, Goddard
Space Flight Center, 18, JPL/DLR, 26 right, JPL/University of Arizona,
26 left, JPL-Caltech, 19, JPL-Caltech/SETI Institute, 27, JPL-Caltech/SSI/
GSFC, 14; Science Source: Lionel Bret, 9, SCIENCE PHOTO LIBRARY, 15;
Shutterstock: alexaldo, 25, berni0004, Cover, Chanchai phetdikhai, 28,
Christos Georghiou, 8, David Hribar, Back Cover, 1, delcarmat, 7, Dotted
Yeti, Cover left, elRoce, 21, Ilia Baksheev, 24, Nostalgia for Infinity, 10, Orla,
6, pio3, 13, Tragoolchitr Jittasaiyapan, 22, Vadim Sadovski, 5, 17

Design Elements
Shutterstock: Arcady, BLACKDAY, ebes, LynxVector, phipatbig, Stefan
Holm, veronchick_84

Editorial Credits
Editor: Kristen Mohn; Designer: Jennifer Bergstrom; Media Researcher:
Tracy Cummins; Production Specialist: Tori Abraham

All internet sites appearing in back matter were available and accurate
when this book was sent to press.

Printed in the United States of America.
PA117

Table of Contents

Words in **bold** are in the glossary.

Jupiter, Big and Bright

Jupiter is very bright. Only the moon and Venus are brighter in the night sky. Jupiter is easy to see. It is one of five **planets** you can see with the naked eye. People have known about Jupiter for thousands of years.

Jupiter is made of some of the same things as the sun. If Jupiter were larger, it could have become a star!

There are eight planets in our **solar system**. Jupiter is the biggest one. About 1,300 Earths could fit inside it!

Jupiter gets its name from Roman myths. Jupiter was king of the gods. He was also god of thunder and lightning. Jupiter's symbol is a lightning bolt.

Circling and Spinning

Jupiter is the fifth planet from the sun. Earth is the third planet. Planets move in a circle around the sun. This path is called an **orbit**.

Earth takes one year to circle the sun. Jupiter takes 12 Earth years to circle the sun!

Jupiter in orbit

Planets also spin during orbit. Jupiter spins quickly. It spins one time in 10 hours. That means its day is only 10 hours long! A day on Earth is 24 hours.

Jupiter's fast spin changes its shape. Its top and bottom are flatter. Its middle part pushes out. The planet is not quite round. It looks like a ball that has lost some air.

The Great Gas Giant

Some planets are called **gas giants**. They are planets that are made up of **gases**. Jupiter is the largest gas giant. Its top layer is made of gas.

Saturn is a gas giant too. Some people also call Neptune and Uranus gas giants. Others call them ice giants.

Imagine you weigh 50 pounds (23 kilograms) on Earth. You would weigh 127 pounds (58 kg) on Jupiter. But Jupiter has no ground to stand on!

Gases swirling around Jupiter

Gas and ice push down toward the center of the planet. This pushing creates **pressure**. Pressure makes the gases very hot and thick. The gases are like soup deep inside Jupiter.

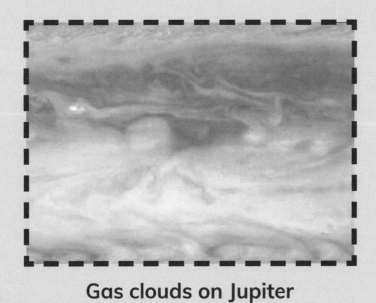

Gas clouds on Jupiter

Jupiter's core

Jupiter is made of more than just gases. There is a rocky **core** at its center. It is very hot there. The core is a little bigger than Earth. It weighs about 20 times more than Earth!

Fuzzy Atmosphere

Jupiter has gas clouds. The clouds look fuzzy. This is because Jupiter spins so quickly. The clouds are part of Jupiter's **atmosphere**. Scientists believe there might be water in some of these clouds.

Jupiter's gas clouds give the planet its color. It looks white, orange, brown, and red.

People look through **telescopes** to study planets. We have learned many things about Jupiter using telescopes. But Jupiter's thick clouds are hard to see through.

Jupiter's rings

Jupiter has four rings around it.
Saturn has much brighter rings.
They are easier to see than Jupiter's.

A **probe** sent pictures of Jupiter's
rings back to Earth. The rings are
made up of small bits of dust. There
are also tiny moons in these rings.

Some scientists think it rains diamonds in Jupiter's atmosphere! They might fall like hail. But we don't know for sure.

Probe flying by Jupiter

Wild Weather on Jupiter

Jupiter has really bad weather. Its top layer is covered in strong storms. The storms are like Earth's hurricanes. The winds on Jupiter blow at very high speeds.

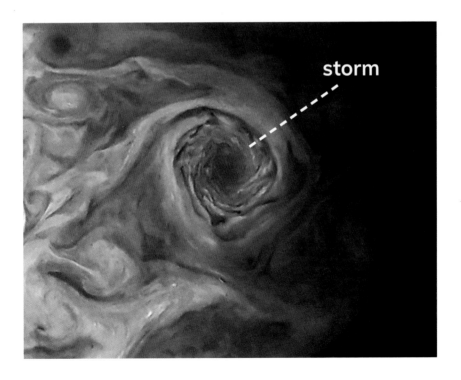

storm

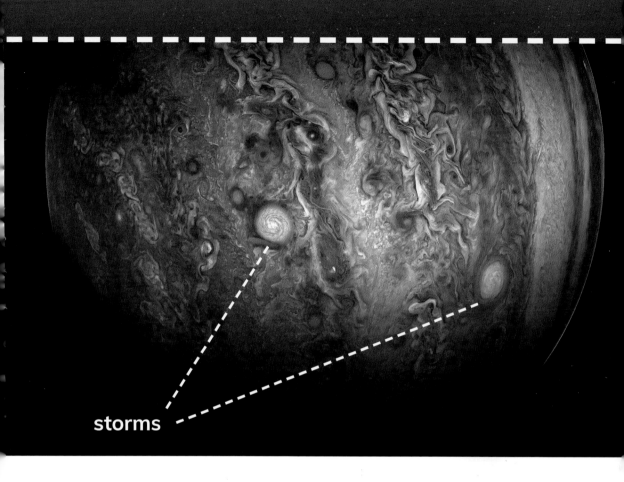

storms

Jupiter has lightning. It is very bright. It may be 1,000 times stronger than lightning on Earth.

Some of Jupiter's storms can last hundreds of years!

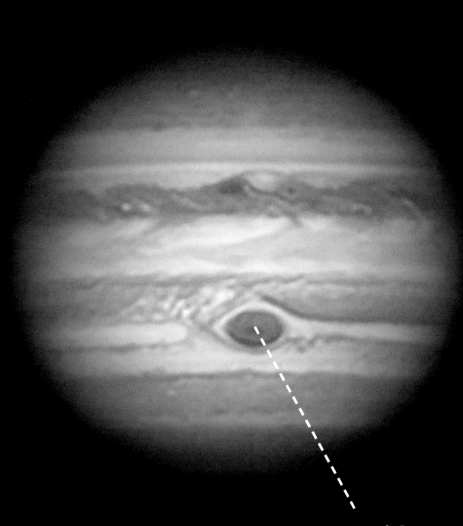

Jupiter's Great Red Spot

Jupiter's largest storm is called the Great Red Spot. It is a hurricane that has lasted at least 350 years. This storm is bigger than Earth!

Jupiter has small storms too. They can become part of larger storms. Not long ago, three small storms joined. They made a large storm called the Little Red Spot. It is smaller than the Great Red Spot.

Jupiter's Many Moons

Earth has one moon. Jupiter has at least 79! Many of its moons don't have names yet. In the 1600s, Galileo Galilei studied Jupiter. He discovered four of Jupiter's largest moons. These moons are Ganymede, Io, Callisto, and Europa.

statue of Galieo Galilei

Ganymede is the largest moon in the solar system. It is larger than Mercury. If this moon orbited the sun, it would be a planet.

Io is very colorful. It is covered in volcanoes. Io goes around Jupiter in an oval shape.

Callisto seems dark and quiet. Some people call it a "dead moon." But large oceans may be hiding under its top layers.

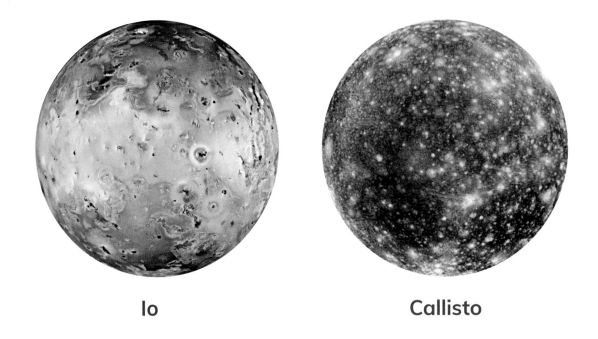

Io   Callisto

Europa

Europa has a large, salty sea. It is covered in ice. Many people think this moon may have life on it. If aliens exist, they may be here!

Nine probes have taken pictures of Jupiter. Someday we may be able to send probes into Jupiter's gas clouds. That would help us learn more about the planet.

Maybe one day, you will help discover new facts about our solar system's largest planet!

Fast Facts

Name:
Jupiter

Location:
5th planet from the sun

Planet Type:
gas giant

Discovered:
Ancient people spotted bright Jupiter in the night sky. Nicolaus Copernicus determined that Jupiter was a planet in the 1600s.

Moons:
79

Glossary

atmosphere (AT-muh-sfeer)—the layer of gases around some planets, dwarf planets, and moons

core (KOR)—the inner part of a planet or a dwarf planet that is made of metal or rock

gas (GASS)— something that is not solid or liquid and does not have a definite shape

gas giant (GASS JYE-unt)—a large planet made up mostly of gases

ice giant (ICE JYE-unt)—a planet made up mostly of ice and liquids

orbit (OR-bit)—the path an object follows while circling an object in space

planet (PLAN-it)—a large object that moves around a star

pressure (PRESH-ur)—the force made by pressing on something

probe (PROHB)—a small vehicle used to explore objects in outer space

solar system (SOH-lur SISS-tuhm)—the sun and the objects that move around it

telescope (TEL-uh-skohp)—a tool people use to look at objects in space

volcano (vol-KAY-noh)—an opening in a planet's surface that sometimes sends out hot lava, steam, and ash

Read More

Baines, Becky. *Planets*. Washington, D.C.: National Geographic Kids, 2016.

Bloom, J.P. *Jupiter*. North Mankato, MN: Capstone Classroom, 2017.

Rathburn, Betsy. *Jupiter*. Minneapolis: Bellwether Media, 2019.

Internet Sites

10 Facts about Space!
https://www.natgeokids.com/nz/discover/science/space/ten-facts-about-space/

Jupiter Facts for Kids
http://www.sciencekids.co.nz/sciencefacts/planets/jupiter.html

NASA Kids' Club
https://www.nasa.gov/kidsclub/index.html

Index